WE WILL SING!

Performance Program One

by Doreen Rao

Assisting Authors:
Lori-Anne Dolloff
Sandra Prodan

BOOSEY & HAWKES

AN IMAGEM COMPANY

DISTRIBUTED BY

HAL•LEONARD®
CORPORATION
7777 W. BLUEMOUND RD. P.O. BOX 13819 MILWAUKEE, WI 53213

The following materials are available for the *We Will Sing!* series:

Table of Contents

The page numbers listed under the Orientation and Rehearsal Guide headings above refer to the corresponding pages in the *We Will Sing!* textbook (TXB 81), sold separately.

Orientation

O Music, Sweet Music
Lowell Mason (1792 – 1872)

Pitch

Vocal Line: Conjunct stepwise motion developed around: *do - re - mi - fa - so*

Tonality: G major (Begins *do - re - mi*)

Phrase Structure: Three 4-bar phrases (4 + 4 + 4)

Texture: Unison song with piano accompaniment (optional canon version in three parts)

Vocal Range:

Time

Meter: Duple

Meter Signature: $\frac{2}{2}$

Conduct: In 2

Tempo: ($\downarrow$ = ca. 112)

Characteristic Rhythm:

Performance Timing: ca. 2′ 30″

Text

Source: Lowell Mason

Theme: Festive school song celebrating music and inviting the chorus to sing.

Form

Unison version organized in three 4-bar phrases; may be sung in two- or three-part canon.

Style

19th century American school song written for the purpose of motivating and inspiring students to sing.

Social - Historical

Lowell Mason was America's first public school music teacher known for his ability in hymn singing and conducting choirs. In 1838, Mr. Mason convinced the Boston schools to include singing as an essential part of the school curriculum.

O MUSIC
VERSION 1
Unison Voices with Piano Accompaniment

LOWELL MASON
Arranged by Doreen Rao

O MUSIC
VERSION 2
Canon in two or three parts*

LOWELL MASON
Arranged by Doreen Rao

O__ mu - sic, sweet _ mu - sic, thy __ prais - es we will

sing; we _ will _ tell of the _ plea - sures and _ hap - pi - ness you _

bring. Mu - sic, mu - sic, let the cho - rus sing.

O__ mu - sic, sweet _ mu - sic, thy __ prais - es we will

sing; we __ will __ tell of the __ plea - sures and __

O __ mu - sic, sweet_ mu - sic, thy __

* The version in canon may be performed unaccompanied, or with the keyboard accompaniment of the unison version.

Orientation

The Sally Gardens

Irish Tune, arr. Benjamin Britten
(1913 – 1976)

Pitch

Vocal Line: Conjunct

Tonality: D♭ major (Begins *do - re - mi*)

Phrase Structure: Each of the two melodically identical verses is made up of four 4-bar phrases

Texture: Unison voices and piano; distinct piano accompaniment; repeated eighth-note chords played in the right hand; melodic motives played in the left hand

Vocal Range:

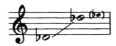

Time

Meter: Duple

Meter Signature: $\frac{2}{2}$

Conduct: In 4

Tempo: Commodo (♩ = 66)

Characteristic Rhythm:

Performance Time: 2' 35"

Text

Source: Poem by William Butler Yeats (1874-1939) first published in 1908 in *Collected Poems of W.B. Yeats.*

Theme: Unhappy love

Form

Strophic form with two stanzas:
[Intro (4), A (4+4), B (4+4), A (4), interlude (4), A (4+4), B (4), A (4), Code (4)]

Style

Traditional Irish song distinctly set in contemporary style by the celebrated English composer Benjamin Britten; carefully detailed dynamics and staccato articulations help distinguish and contrast a long, legato vocal line with a more rhythmically active accompaniment figure.

Social - Historical

Irish songs often tell stories of life and love; favorite songs are passed down from generation to generation from parent to child, and from friend to friend. Benjamin Britten had a great love of folk songs. He regularly used their melodic themes in both his instrumental and vocal writing.

To Clytie Mundy

THE SALLY GARDENS

Irish Tune

*Words by**
W.B. YEATS

Arranged by
BENJAMIN BRITTEN

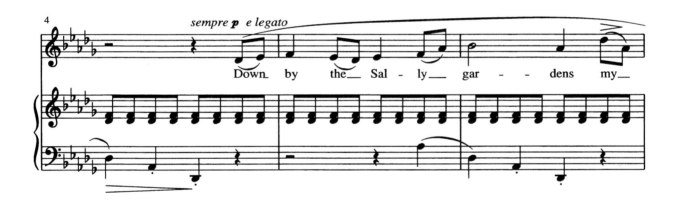

WINTHROP ROGERS EDITION
© Copyright 1958 by Boosey & Co., Ltd. Copyright Renewed. All rights reserved.

*The words of this song are reprinted from "Collected Poems of W.B. Yeats" by permission of Mrs. Yeats.

Orientation

Simple Gifts

Shaker Song, arr. Aaron Copland
(1900 – 1990)

Pitch

Vocal Line: Dance-like, conjunct, mostly step-wise

Tonality: A♭ major (begins *so. - do*)

Phrase Structure: Four 4-bar phrases

Texture: Unison voices with piano accompaniment

Vocal Range:

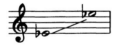

Time

Meter: Duple

Meter Signature: ²⁄₄

Conduct: In 2

Tempo: (♩ = 72)

Characteristic Rhythm:

Performance Time: 1′ 25″

Text

Source: Shaker hymn

Theme: Simplicity and humility; thanksgiving and joy.

Form

Three-part form: [Intro (2), A (4+4), Interlude (2), B (4+5), Interlude (2), A (4+4), Coda (4)]

Style

The setting is contemporary, "popular" style and tonal; recognized as characteristically American.

Social - Historical

Simple Gifts is selected from Aaron Copland's collection *Old American Songs.* Copland's arrangements of these familiar songs are often performed by solo voice and orchestra. The *Shaker Song* can also be heard in theme and variations in Copland's orchestral suite, *Appalachian Spring,* a ballet he wrote for the beloved American choreographer, Martha Graham.

SIMPLE GIFTS

Arranged by
AARON COPLAND

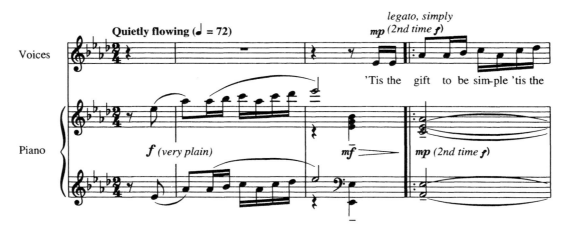

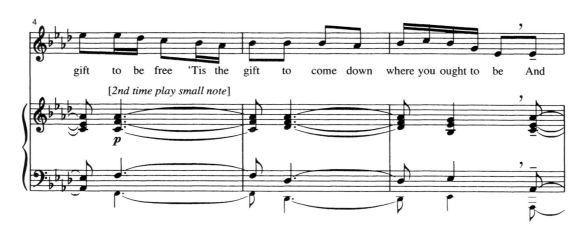

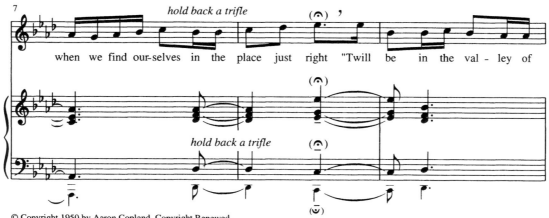

Orientation

She's Like the Swallow
Newfoundland folksong
arr: Lori-Anne Dolloff

Pitch

Vocal Line: Mostly conjunct, some chordal skips, especially *mi - la*

Tonality: d minor (Begins: *la . - mi*)

Phrase Structure: Four 4-bar phrases

Texture: Unison voices, piano accompaniment, flute obligato

Vocal Range:

Time

Meter: Triple

Meter Signature: ¾

Conduct: In 1 or 3

Tempo: (♩ = 104)

Characteristic Rhythm:

Performance Time: 2′ 45″

Text

Source: From Newfoundland, the eastern most Province of Canada; part of a longer song with many verses; each verse has four lines rhyming A - A - B - B.

Theme: Lamenting; telling of a young maid who dies brokenhearted from the difficulties of life; song of love, longing, and regret.

Form

Strophic with three verses and a repeat of the first verse: [A, A′, A″, A]; the text and accompaniment figure change from verse to verse.

Style

Folksong style; like many folksongs, *She's Like the Swallow* tells a sad story; text is the constantly changing element therefore text is central to the interpretation; the character of the performance should reflect the longing and sadness of the text in relation to the minor tonality.

Social - Historical

One of the most beautiful and well known Newfoundland songs, this arrangement was written especially for classroom choirs. Its has been varied here with the use of triple meter, piano, and flute obligato. Some versions of this song are notated in compound duple meter (⁶⁄₈).

SHE'S LIKE THE SWALLOW

Arranged by
LORI-ANNE DOLLOFF

rose. The more she plucked, the more she pulled, un - til she

got ___ her a - pron full.

Slower (♩ = 72)

l.h.
mp poco marcato

'Twas out of those ros - es she made a bed, A ston - y

mp

pp

mp

pil - low for her head. She laid her down, _ no word she

spoke, Un - til this fair _ maid's heart _ was broke

She's like the swal - low that flies so

Orientation

A Spring Morning
Henry Carey (1687 – 1743)

Pitch

Vocal Line: Lilting, dance-like, mostly conjunct, organized in scale-like passages and sequences

Tonality: E♭ major with modulation to g minor (begins *so - la*)

Phrase Structure: 4-bar phrases throughout

Texture: Unison voices, piano accompaniment

Vocal Range:

Time

Meter: Triple

Meter Signature: ¾ (felt in 1)

Conduct: In 3 or 1

Tempo: Moderato, (about ♩ = 132)

Characteristic Rhythm:

Performance Time: ca. 2′ 10″

Text

Source: A pastoral theme imitating bird calls, piping, singing, and springing; on the subject of nature and love.

Theme: Originally published as "A Pastoral" in 1899, words in this version by H. Lane Wilson, originally published by Boosey & Co. in 1902.

Form

Ternary, A B A da capo: [Intro, A (8+8), A′ (8+4), Interlude, B (8+8), Interlude, A (8+8), Coda]

Style

Pastoral song style, word painting devices to represent bird calls and piping sounds; melismatic passages vocalized on one syllable "ah" contrasting with the predominantly syllabic style; light and dance-like, with the feeling of one pulse per measure.

Social - Historical

Henry Carey was an English composer, poet, playwright, and librettist, who spent most of his career in London writing popular songs like the famous "Sally in our Alley." He rarely used his first name, just "Mr. Carey" appears on his manuscripts.

A SPRING MORNING

A Pastoral

HENRY CAREY
Edited by Doreen Rao

1. Flocks are sport - ing, doves are court - ing, Warb- ling
2. Danc- ing, sing - ing, pip - ing, spring - ing, With our

Orientation

Good Night

Dmitri Kabalevsky (1904 – 1987)

Pitch

Vocal Line: Descending 2-bar motive followed by an ascending sequence climaxing at the octave.

Tonality: d minor (begins on *mi*)

Phrase Structure: 4-bar phrases

Texture: Unison voices (optional two-part), piano

Vocal Range:

Time

Meter: Duple

Meter Signature: $\frac{2}{4}$

Conduct: In 2

Tempo: Larghetto, (ca. ♩ = 66)

Characteristic Rhythm:

Performance Time: ca. 1′ 45″

Text

Source: Taught to Doreen Rao by Dmitri Kabalevsky in 1966 as a symbol of their friendship.

Theme: Lullaby assuring a child that night is coming and it is time to sleep; translated into English from Russian.

Pronunciation:

Russian Word	IPA Symbol	Translation
Spakoinyi	[spɑkoinyi]	Good
notsi	[nɔtʃi]	Night

Form

Binary A B A B: [Intro (4), A (4+4), B (4+8), Interlude (4), A (4+4), B (4+8), Coda (5)]

Style

In the character of a Russian lullaby, a swaying, rocking, legato line imaging the scene of a mother rocking her child; simple and in hushed tones.

Social - Historical

Composer Dmitri Kabalevsky is best known for his instrumental compositions, especially his piano works for students. But his fame in Russia centers around his vocal writing and philosophy of music education. Doreen Rao's arrangement for young choirs was first performed at the American Orff Schulwerk National Conference in Chicago in November 1987 by the Glen Ellyn Children's Chorus. The arrangement is dedicated to Mr. Kabalevsky's memory for his life-long commitment to the music education of children throughout the world.

GOOD NIGHT

DMITRI KABALEVSKY
Arranged by Doreen Rao